Invention *of* *the* Wilderness

Invention *of*
the Wilderness

POEMS

Bruce Bond

LOUISIANA STATE UNIVERSITY PRESS

BATON ROUGE

Published by Louisiana State University Press
lsupress.org

LSU Press Paperback Original

Designer: Barbara Neely Bourgoyne
Typeface: Whitman

Cover illustration: *The Pool*, by Aron Wiesenfeld. Courtesy of the artist.

Thanks to the following journals, in which some of these poems first appeared: *Birmingham Poetry Review, Blackbird, Boston Review, Cimarron Review, Crazyhorse, Literary Matters, MĀNOA: A Pacific Journal of International Writing, North American Review, Pedestal, Prairie Schooner, Raritan, The Red Letter, South Florida Poetry Journal, Stand,* and *Tupelo Quarterly.* Thanks as well to Seven Kitchens Press for publishing the poem "Arrow" as a chapbook.

Library of Congress Cataloging-in-Publication Data

Names: Bond, Bruce, 1954– author.
Title: Invention of the wilderness : poems / Bruce Bond.
Description: Baton Rouge : Louisiana State University Press, [2022]
Identifiers: LCCN 2022005030 (print) | LCCN 2022005031 (ebook) | ISBN
  978-0-8071-7796-9 (paperback) | ISBN 978-0-8071-7863-8 (pdf) | ISBN
  978-0-8071-7862-1 (epub)
Subjects: LCGFT: Poetry.
Classification: LCC PS3552.O5943 I58 2022 (print) | LCC PS3552.O5943
  (ebook) | DDC 811/.54—dc23/eng/20220204
LC record available at https://lccn.loc.gov/2022005030
LC ebook record available at https://lccn.loc.gov/2022005031

innocence, the destroyer of wildness;
wildness, the victim of an idea that says
virtue is denial, betrayal
of the too-full fullness of the world;
the pretty skater featured like flawless ice.

—DONALD REVELL

CONTENTS

I.

Eco

The other member of this conversation
is the forest we are in, the one that is here

and not quite here, not the woods we knew
when we were young and lost and elsewhere.

I too have a new face and the faceless wound
it floats on, the long loneliness for power

to salvage some broken friend or ocean.
Just when I thought I was alone, again,

my limbs take on the look of skies on fire,
as planets do, and monks, and drunken men

whose vague unease is longing to be shared.
Even the best convictions dream the damaged

world that says, I know, I too am worried.
The other voice among us is a certain change

in the wind. And once, when I was young,
I heard it speak. And in its speaking, listen.

Islands of the Arctic

The oldest ices are the first to decline,
　　　　the least hardened by salts of the modern

ocean and so the first to be forgotten,
　　　　to carry the international waters ashore.

Imagine an amnesia that takes the core
　　　　and cortex of the long gone and leaves us

nameless, spacing out between commercials.
　　　　First ice, then grief, then the letting go,

as if the polar regions where they weep
　　　　belong to no one, their foothold tenuous,

their boundaries political and therefore challenged.
　　　　Or that they liquefy to the vast unease

whose waves are everywhere and nowhere clear,
　　　　whose siren strikes the coastal town that braces

for rage. Or something more impersonal.
　　　　Those who lose a loved one's mind, long

before it takes the body with it, they know
　　　　that look, the inconsolable note of danger

in eyes whose hidden wires are condemned.
　　　　Or the fight in the evicted memory,

the man in the man who says to his wife,
what have you done with my wife. And why.

I have seen it, and yet I have not seen it
coming or where it goes, or known the words

to answer the garbled phone call in the night.
First ice, then dread, then the shore inhaling

the drowned islands of the Arctic we call
a continent. Or sea. Or one day neither.

It's here, they say, the deep past becoming
deeper, the nation smaller, the real estate

more priceless, just before the market tanks,
and who can tell what it will make us,

each on the raft of her rooftop waiting
for an answer, a copter, the deus ex

machina of fresh water and supplies.
Who will save the harbor where the seas turn

to one sea, one great infusion, surge on surge
of paradise washing through our wetlands,

our walls, our questioning, who, whose home
is this, this blur we stand on, searching the sky.

Paradise

When a tree falls and no one is there, it falls
into the earth below. I hear it. I hear it again.

In my last picture of Lisa, we are drinking
coffee and she says, my mind keeps going

off into the future. What if it is nothing.
She is bald, pale as birch, and her worried beauty

shadows my cup and version of that word: *nothing.*
In a smaller picture we are children together,

almost in love, awkward with unspoken things.
I thought it came to nothing, and here we are, drinking,

decades later, making plans for an autumn
without leaves. Or people. She has a fridge full of pot,

she laughs, *medicine,* and I do not see,
behind her quick charmed eye, the many trees on fire.

Or if she sees. I do not hear them as she leaves
for the subway tunnel, having said the thing

we never said, the otherworldly in the word
love that does not, cannot, happen. Perhaps it did.

Long ago in silence. And in the sound, again,
of branches falling, where there are none at all.

Lakes of the Southern Plains

The numbers of the drowned are up this year.
      We know because we count them, chart them,

with or without the evidence dragged ashore.
      The numbers inside the numbers tell stories

without an end. No casket save now
      and then the empty box a couple lowers.

They say the majority of children wander off
      unattended five minutes or less. They say

the usual victim makes no noise, no gesture.
      They say a lot, and no one knows just why

the numbers, why these lakes in particular.
      Did the flooded trees beneath the surface

catch the swimmer unaware or breed there
      the grappling hooks of weeds among the branches.

I heard that once, and now I keep seeing
      what no one can unless, perhaps, they're drowning.

Are the depths too close, winds too strong,
      however slight the visible disturbance.

When I think of lakes of the southern plains,
      I think of stillness mostly. And yet I know

just this year a man dove in at high noon
      to get back something. Just what he lost,

the papers did not say, only that it drifted
      on the subtext of some current, unforeseen.

Farther and farther, and somewhere I imagine
      he encountered some reversal of desire,

or perhaps he had no chance, having reached
      his last stroke, his obscure object floating

over the deeper reaches, as stories do
      and those they hope to caution or reclaim.

Niagara

And then the husband, head bowed, eyes closed,
    a tourist pamphlet in his lap, says,

did you know the green color of the water
    is the color of the falls coming to an end.

And the bride says, you do not look good, love,
    pale as an angel. Are you sleeping well,

eating well. Did you know, he says,
    sixty tons of salt and rock flour drain

each minute, a foot each year, and in a thousand
    lifetimes, there will be no falls at all.

And the bride takes the pamphlet from his hands
    and folds it tenderly as if it were a thing

she loved and worried over. Did you know,
    he says on the verge of sleep that never arrives,

the end of his sentence carried out to sea.
    And the rainbow comes and goes according

to the clouds. And when it comes, the petals
    of the cameras open, as they did just now.

And somewhere in a stranger's photograph,
    the man turns to the woman and says, did you

know. And she says, no, dear, I did not.
    Or was it, yes, I did. Either way

her palm on his brow is a bridal veil
    of water. It cures the sleepless, that sound.

It is the angel in the downpour, the coin
    so old it passes faceless through our hands.

And with that, the couple vanishes.
    And a monument of mist rises. And falls.

Coyote
Elegy for W. S. Merwin

I knew a man who cut his chest each night
       to let the animal scamper out,

alone, and sniff the corners of the dark,
       until it had no corner, no harbor,

no name, only an aurora of smoke
       about the creature whose breath

shadowed the emptiness, so long as the man
       whose heart it was could breathe.

I never knew another who felt as close
       to those quick as a candle to flicker out

at first sight, or eat, in stealth, his berries.
       I want to say, with each departure,

a wound closed, a question opened,
       though I know this is, at best, half-true.

If he filled with cautionary wonder,
       he filled the way a well fills with voices

foreign to wells, or the gulches of the south
       with the rain of a distant county.

So long as he was breathing, he would hear
       in the throats of hills the sirens

of some home emergency coyotes know
    only by its howl, forgotten

until now, and by the beacon's arrow
    through the canyon of the blind facades,

the light that cut, blood, lock, and sternum,
    to save the beast they cried for.

A Tower in the Woods

Seasonal fires wherever they may find us,
        here at the edge of the northern forest,

lit at point of origin by cloud, crash,
        or high-voltage cable; they blaze a path

so remote our rangers watch and wait
        atop their towers for the rain to break

and smoke to draw a curtain on the fury.
        A curse to any one tree, but to the many

an angel's rage to liquidate the resin,
        to scorch the cone and seedpod open.

Even as the dead wood falls and birds
        wing the smoke in horrified numbers,

the sound you hear is the larger picture
        that tears itself to pieces, that takes fear

and accident and animal cry and makes
        of them a structure. Whatever the heartache

or careless cigarette, it hacks the lock
        on some great secret, buried, banned, lost

on each, until, that is, we see the forest
        in the tree. It is one thing to outlast

a reign of terror, another to require it,
        to take its energy as yours. The sticks

and needles and crucibles of decay
      trees need, they likewise need to clear away.

Flames become one flame, the holler of *fire*
      one fever across the crowded theater.

Each rain one rain, and because you listen,
      the broken bits of sky that make it rain.

How this comforts, I do not understand,
      but there it is, the sound of fracture that holds

a squall together, that polishes the glass
      heart of each light sleeper, each forest guest

come to this. The crackle of these leaves,
      this thunder, the fading of the long stampede.

Redactions from the Last Debate

When I was a child, one eye went blind
and then, in sympathy, the other.

Twins again with their own twin code.
Scissors, with your spectacles, tell me,

are they open or closed. Are you no
less eyeless, the moment you are used.

Was that you at my window, the chirp
of the screw that holds your blades together.

Was it God who said, let there be light,
and darkness fell like a head into a basket.

Like a floe in the arctic with a heap of cellular phones.
I fear we fear the wrong connections.

The earth on the radio blows a plume
of smoke into the room, blackening the ceiling.

The flies in the ice cap long to be released.
What is any fly without the open air,

any blade of grass without the pasture.
When I swear that I am here, the field

there, wind everywhere among the shivers,
a slant of light through the window casts

a thousand tiny threads, a thousand hooks.
I see them, cut them, and the oceans rise.

II.

Arrow

Straight lines in rocks are common,
  in plants rare, in animals nowhere

   to be seen, save in the space
that sees, spirit shot through

  the eye like light into a crystal.
   Days after she spoke her final word,

my mother looked dead
  ahead, unflinching. Vigilant or blind,

   we could not say, or know
the measure of our mercies

  that drew a curtain on the garden.
   Her eye, I thought, was one horizon

I never cross. I told myself,
  she was on a straight path. Somewhere.

   As those who look into the fog
walk a step ahead of what they see.

  The street in a slow immolation of mist.
   One morning as a child.

2.

Each year a Jahrzeit completes its return
        the way a sun completes its arc into the sea.

            The closing of the circle is the moment
of eclipse. Each night a mother reads

        to a boy. To recall is to forget
            just enough to make the journey.

To forget is to forget. The moon
        in the lantern of the iris, the sun

            in the iris of the moon. They are waiting
on a name for what they are in each other:

        the two as one, the one as one
            dissolving. Any boy will tell you,

a separate room is gold. A separate voice above the well
        that speaks in deepened voices.

            Each day the year pushes a lingering
heat through the light we see.

        A mother pushes a child into day.
            The flash of the camera pierces the bride.

3.

But we are children of forbearance still.
    Exhaustion bends

        our backs into puzzles, our paths
into gardens in the cities of our youth.

      The curvature of the river
        undoes the silks of the human eye:

sun into water, black
      into the pupil's blackening pond.

      We are children
of the koi and willow that grieve no thing, no one.

      The architects of cities
        must have known a thing

about exhaustion, how streets long to bend
      against their parks and rivers.

      The crackle of departure,
it waters the eye. It makes the sound

      of wind and leaves. In each
        the name for the other, the silence of both.

4.

She who gave me words gave me
        this. A calendar of empty spaces,

                the measures of a childhood,
inaudible now, gone

                cold and still as music when it listens.
                When I was small,

the silence of words before I spoke
        was monstrous. And who am I to know.

                I talk of things I cannot see,
because I am their child.

                The picture book I love is older than me.
                Older still,

the child's need, large lettered and alone.
        Over and over. When are you coming home,

                my mother asked.
She who gave me language gave me this.

        The smoke of mouths
                speaking in the cold.

5.

The words are out there,
    the long-adored and thereby damaged

        Robinson Crusoe your mother left.
Its margins illegible now. A voice

      laid over the voice laid over the sea
        that claps its bracelet to your ankles

and pulls. You read it long ago
    but never with these small reminders,

        her hand so experienced, her self-notes
so rapidly drawn in waves, by weariness

      bent on their own erasure.
        And the ocean becomes a name for that.

A name for the nameless souls at sea.
    Which brings you to the edge of sleep,

        and your lips begin to move.
Are you aware. Do you hear the castaway reading

      as you read. Do you see your body
        listing in the harbor. As you are told.

6.

The pistil, the cup, the burr of pollen,
     of bee.

       They seed the eye
and bloom a little longer. A mother tweezers the stinger

     from a boy's hand
         and yet the sting remains.

Beneath the kiss. Unseen. The terrible
     surprise of being. Alone. Look,

       says the child.
Look, reply the many objects in the room.

     The lamp, the crayon,
         the ball, the names that remind us

what use they serve,
     what good. The bee sizzles somewhere.

       I see, the mother
says to her child. Somewhere out there the earth

     grows dark. Beyond the ghost
         reflection in the darkening glass.

7.

The wind, the leaves,
  together they make the sound of a roof

  on fire. The sound
of listening. The two made one and ever torn apart.

  I want to believe I was closer
    to things before I spoke of them.

Take this music,
  this ordinary eye glassed in amazement.

  The slow sure invention
of amazement. If the arrow of a song pinned me

  as a child, who am I to know.
    Where there is wonder, there is smoke.

There is a childhood burning in the distance.
  Where there are blossoms,

  the simplifying word:
blossom. The way it longs to join the others.

  The many blossoms in
    one word. Survive the death of each.

8.

The breath, the word, the continual
        loss of one to the other, the flight of the arrow

                that bends, in time, slowly to the earth.
Any grave will tell you.

                We write on our tombs the long birth names
                        foreign to our friends.

As if the soul were a formal
        stranger, a funeral hymn, a vault to stave

                the emptiness.
I too came back to earth with the help of a strong chorale.

                It mastered nothing. I am in its debt.
                It was the wounded body

I learned to leave alone.
        In the distance the sound of the reception

                was hopeful.
My mother left a bench in her name. Every night it empties.

                Every autumn it lights the emptiness
                        on fire.

9.

A mother is a mother
    always, and never the woman she was.

        Must experience come to light
only in the act of burning.

        A dead man is a man
            the way the silence after music

is music. And then, in time, less and less.
        And what do you expect of an inner life.

        Figures
drawn like breath. And so let go. Long ago

        my mother gave me the word *death*
            and changed it

to *passed on*. I use the phrase without thinking,
        without knowing how

        it works.
Dear hope. I am asking. Do we have a word

        for what never quite arrives.
            Never leaves.

10.

The violence of the chisel leaves
    a calm beneath the shadows of the garden.

    A break from the curvature
of rivers. Straight lines in rocks are common

    to rocks though rare enough
        in the wilderness to hunt the eye.

Beneath a shattered bowl of crows,
    the cry that says, here we are, again,

    never saying who. From a distance,
the many graves of Veteran's Park

    are one great adagio of stone.
    Some of them are read, reread,

only to fall in line with the others,
    each with its nameless flutter of stars.

    The great design
deepens the calm, the formality of footstep,

    the gravity that pins a number
    to the field.

II.

If you drop a wing in a pool of water,
    the ripple widens to an eye

        and the fish rise, and when one leaps
in hunger, it breaks glass,

    a sleeper wakes, the grief of being,
        once again, adrift, washes over,

and she is looking for a pill, a thing
    to take away the thought

        of what, do not ask, of nothing,
she answers, nothing before this

    earth, nothing after, fish scatter
        and do not ask, then the leaves,

the storm is coming, and the sky says
    nothing and who would know,

        what heaven says it says to the mirror,
she drinks, she swallows, her face

    goes under the darkening
        cloud, and the feeding never ends.

12.

My mother had three names once, then four,
   then hundreds

         in the picture books that darkened
as she spoke. The stories she read

      were one story
         where she is reading to a child.

What anxiety does not multiply,
      it divides. What it does not bend, it straightens.

            Straight lines in sentences are common,
in the wilderness rare, in the literal heart

      nowhere to be seen.
            When we give a child a name,

we give a name an overflow of needs.
      When we read a story,

            we send an arrow through the darkness.
This inarable wilderness, asks the councilman,

      what good is it, what use. What good are you,
            the wilderness replies.

13.

I too post the words of famous strangers
        on my pages, pictures

            of the beloved
whose death was famous. Repeated without end.

            Here I am, says the home
                turned museum turned a hundred words

that lean a little closer to say,
        history is lonely. The pen Keats left on a desk,

            the slow river
of lead and glass overlooking the yard.

        They need you, use you.
            Love puts things in boxes

when we are young. My mother collected boxes,
        put nothing in them,

            the way calendars put days in homes.
When my mother died, I asked,

        Is this happening,
            world. I asked myself. Is this.

14.

My mother liked to ask the same questions
          over and over.

                    Like a music box that plays
only when it's closed.

               When will you be
                    home. Should I take this pill.

The answer was always a step
          beyond the step in the fog.

                    Pushed or pulled
or both. Like music that way. Or wind.

               The crackle of autumn
                    against the window.

Do not call her weak. Or curse the temerity
          that affirms no thing.

                    The winded machinery
of hope that sings its one note in the storm.

               To be the unknowing and a thing
                    apart. A listening.

15.

What in the music of the question unsettles
        what it calms.

            What in the broken
bowl of crows that rise. And in a question's

            proximity to silence,
                its need for company.

Where better to host a heaven
        but the air. The long and tender

            cruelties of our final measures,
the anesthesia that kills,

            odd soft laughter
                exchanged in the hospice:

what are these things
        in light of the calm and violence

            of some great design.
When did the powerless become the better friend.

            Should I take this pill.
                Did I. When will you be home.

16.

In the end, there were books with large letters.
    A lamp and the word *lamp*

        brightest at night.
The wall beside her nightmare was the door

        she walked through years ago.
        When she last spoke.

The sting of light in the hospice room
    is common, the beam

        that splits the tendril into bloom.
We gave her oranges and flowers

        because she had so little space.
        We gave her rivers.

The rose opens, the pupil
    narrows, the stem slips into the hole.

        When I was a kid,
I was stung in a garden like this. By wilderness

        betrayed, invited. Pinned
        to a world I had no words for.

17.

The child listens to the piano explain some things
      about nothing

          long after the piano is gone.
What we make is made

     of fire,
          some of which is coming.

Long ago, my mother repeated the question:
      but what if it is

          nothing. And I heard *no thing*
in *nothing*. And I said something

      I did not quite believe.
          I heard *not yet* in *no thing.*

Sometimes the more merciful music whispers
      so not to wake us.

          It asks,
Is that you, world. And then a drop

      of morphine. (Is that you in there.)
          And then another.

III.

A Brief History of the Human Ear

The long story says the reptilian ear evolved,
      fracturing its bone into the three small bones

that, as separate, fitted, tissue-bound, do the better work
      we do, noting the tinier details of the forest.

Three bones and the shiver of things in the distance
      to rival any jeweler with his monocle,

any watch laid bare to the fine-point tweezer.
      And we are born this way, broken, and so listening

to the other pieces of the puzzle. Remember
      the mobile of stars, how it snowed a little music,

and the music had parts too small to isolate.
      I must have heard them too, not knowing what they were.

I was just a little watch after all. A glint
      in the larger drama. And everything was changing,

breaking, like a stick on fire. And the music
      I took to heart began to shatter into small

and smaller pieces, without ceasing to be music,
      so there would always be something in there

I heard and did not know I heard. Articulate
      as rain. A flute here. A lizard in the ivy.

Crickets

To each its species, its specialty and song:
     ant cricket, field cricket,

the *melodious* versus *tinkling* cricket,
     the *ambitious, confused,*

and among the many *sword crickets*
     the *handsome trig,*

to each the mate who listens for its kind.
     She *understands,* I figure,

but who am I to talk. To cross a line
     I cannot cross to cross

again, to lift a note to those who read
     a foreign music. Lord,

I whisper. Drawn to the small-boned features
     of the garden: the leg,

for one, the cricket's with its barnacles,
     its tympani that listen.

And inside each the fluid of the inner
     cricket, so keen it hears

the feathering of creatures who would eat it.
     The beasts of Eden chafe.

They swallow. The eaters and the eaten fit.
    So says the lord of disorder.

So too the chafe of spirits that likewise fit
    the conflicts of an age.

So many species of danger, a cricket stills
    when you get too close.

When you get too close, the plural of *species*
    is a *species* still.

We need a context, a garden, to be clear.
    We need crickets as crickets

need seclusion, or Job in mourning needs
    a kinder master plan.

Consider, Yahweh says, the many creatures
    of the yard: the pistil,

the behemoth, the casting pool, the tooth.
    So what I hear is dark

and full of blessings, and somewhere a cricket
    carries on, unconscious:

to each its species of song. I cannot help it:
    ant cricket, field cricket,

the *melodious,* the *confused.* To each
song a death, a context.

To every context a glimmer in its armor
that sings, *here I am.*

Here, to its mate. And to the deadly birds
of the kingdom: *here.*

Blue

Then the lake holds its mirror
    to the sky

among the leaves and branches
    of the season,

obscurations that make heaven
    a lake with islands,

the tree a land with lakes,
        and the man with his art

one more acolyte trying
        to get the wilderness down.

In fine and finer strokes,
        he multiplies the leaves

and the cracks between,
        where more leaves fall

into the stillness, into the breath
        of the painter,

as he zeros in to work canvas.
        He knows his favorite

oils have a little poison
        but leans because he must.

Winter here may never come again.
        The finishing touch,

it escapes him now, caught
in the promise of the close

and closer arrangement
with light across the water,

the lovely gaps and distortions
the signature

of a more sweetly permeable nature.
Any wonder

men like him come here
to scatter their own ashes,

to consecrate the bridge collapsed
in broken water,

the living mirror of a sky below.
Seers wander the seen,

long in their loneliness for being
there, where the next

brushstroke would eclipse the last.
What was it he dreamt.

The eye in the shallows, just below,
drowned and staring.

But enough of that. The day grows
cold. No. Colder.

The man coughs into his sleeve.
　　The darker it gets the more

he cuts the threads of light to see.
　　Blue pours through the man,

the canvas, the fallen shapes, and soon
　　they are everywhere,

the blue leaves. Soon they are falling,
　　the way old men fall

asleep in the midday sun,
　　to strike the water blind.

Frog

Whenever I approach the frogs,
    after the night sky has drifted

up from the bottom of the pond,
    they all go still, invisible, mute,

as if song were light and silence shadow
    and their fragility my own.

So this is how death must feel,
    leaning in to touch a child's face

who vanishes, as nightmares do,
    before the light can see them.

Far as I know, the frogs are the story
    their chirping tells, and I

believe, seeing at the water's edge
    only stars where I dare not step,

hearing in every corner of the park
    the pulse that dims to take me in.

Atoll

The shovels of the last war here
　　　take on, in time, a phantom life.

All night the slough of rock, steel,
　　　unclaimed bone, the dull heft

and pallor of silt, raised, turned,
　　　released, and raised again as dust.

An island buries what it must.
　　　Long after the ash has settled

over the eyes, after the suns on flags
　　　have burned and longboats resume,

casting their nets across the wreckage,
　　　the spades keep doing what

spades do. The ghost in the machine
　　　of an otherwise peaceful life

worries the earth, burying the dead
　　　in the dead who just keep rising.

Which is why the islanders leave their home
　　　in foreign hands, promised

for their absence the refinement
　　　of a weapon to end all weapons,

to bomb the hell out of heaven
　　　and give it back. And shipped off

into exile for good, tented on a near shore
     with a crate of provisions,

the ocean breeze their only contract,
     they see it: the blooming of suns

that stretch their haloes from the target.
     Twenty-three in all, each

with its prevailing wind. They feel the heat
     on their faces. And in their eyes,

an image of earth, beyond reach
     or recognition, scattered to the open sea.

Wilderness

Elegy for William Stafford

To you, if you are listening,

        I am no one
and so hear things that no one hears.

If a deer leaps from nowhere
    to the road, what it leaves

of the many bleeds into one.
        And for a moment I hear less,

as no one hears. Minus one.
        But know the river is a road

we walk together. We must.
        It crackles with a good star

that burns the name we give it.
        If I come upon your body

in my path, know I will not, cannot,
        leave. Although I travel on.

The Stones of April

When the storm came, we were alone, lost
    before a wall of glass, first rain, then crystal,

then stones that fell in gathering numbers,
    spits of branch and shingle in the crossfire.

When the sirens sounded, we were deep
    in conversation—something about your father,

how memory had left him and the scholar,
    the pillar, the pacifist he was, the quiet

he kept in each home argument he suffered,
    when, among the others, he was most alone.

When the end came, storms followed, wind
    and the winded, tearing at their bandages,

not knowing why, everywhere the seal
    of the wound broken, the fury released,

the winter stillness of the trees cast off.
    It seemed so pointless, looking for the source

of all that rage, that vortex overhead,
    horizontal hail that struck our headlight.

When the greater blindness came, we saw
    a billion eyes come flying out of heaven,

the yard glittering in the new dark age
    of clouds that swept the afternoon in legions.

We might have been strangers in the path
      this late in the season, though familiar enough,

the man who asks his daughter, what have you
      done with my daughter. When the storm came,

we were one part wind, one part tree that gives
      the wind its signature. We were the hand

that shivers in our dotage, in the wild air
      that falls from nowhere, and everywhere we look.

In Venire

The night my house burned down, I asked
    what now, and my mother had no answer.

Her silence frightened me, and so I looked,
    in silence, back, and a wall knelt down.

If souls have bodies in another life, I see hers
    here, young, afraid. And then, the fire.

Out of the dark, a siren. Out of the siren,
    the rotational flash, the men rushing in.

To invent is to *venture inward*, to cross, open,
    abandon, wound. My mother taught me.

The scent of char crystals as I wake.
    A wind-chain crackles from the branches.

I eat a little something. I return, I say.
    But I never return. If souls have bodies

in another life, I see my own standing
    before a tower of light. I do not know

where grief goes, if it goes. When questions
    get tired, they tend to sleep. I do.

Out of ash, embers. Out of fire, a door.
    The ache of leaves crumpling from their hinges.

IV.

Invention of the Wilderness

I.

When a fire pins its banner to the wood,
it reveals something of the wilderness

no wilderness can know, something locked up
in the structure of the branch that longs

to flower, as those who would refrain from pleasure
long to fissure as their eyelids close.

I have had that dream; that dream had me
listen to a sad chorale, and the notes

with their heavy progress to the grave
of Christ took on the slow magnanimous

purpose of thorns and petals and pews in rows.
It hardly has to do with me, this progress,

but there it was in the skull at the center
of a dark that just gets darker as you go.

2.

Any wonder the great observers kept
an eye on the emptiness and, in awe,

mapped the graveyard of the sky, star
by star. They made a schedule of surprises.

A god's dream pinned with fire turned
the vortex of the clock that cannot die.

It marked time in increments foreign
to our times alone and suffered in our

music. The great listeners heard a song
in the spheres as something other than

its passing, not life on earth, but the field
it plows, the paradise. It drew them close:

to see in the scatter the wheel's return,
each breath held like a leaf against a river.

3.

When I walk into the wilderness,
I become two people, one of them

visibly me incarnate, the other some
member of a great disorder, eyeless

as the leaves that rise, and still they see.
Still the rumors of a wisdom I cannot

fathom. When I cannot sleep, I play
Scrabble. As the words click in place,

the other side of them rises like film
in a developing pan. Amazing, how

much, how easily my animals sleep.
When my cat looks in the mirror, he

sees no cat. The season of his illness,
I felt, across my sternum, no cat too.

4.

I was a maker of birds and so I called
them in a language I did not speak.

I worked night and day until the one
was the other, because I had the power.

My heart began to flicker, scared by doors
that closed slow like the eyes of graves.

I asked myself, as your kingdom grows,
do you wake, alone. Does a swallow

cry in the wilderness that is getting
hotter, smaller. Do you smell the scent

of feathers in the fire, because you have
that power. Do you sleep less at night,

more at noon, at work. As you lay down
your heavy tools, does the cage door open.

5.

When a floating casket catches fire,
the eyes on shore water in the smoke.

As if the eye might touch what it sees,
although it never does. It is not fire.

Never the blaze it bears across the lens,
the coffin that pins its signature to ours.

The last of the fuel consumes the fire
and us who watch it happen from a distance.

I am always a step away, in the province
of the unsaid, where the eyes are hung.

I am always out there, in the distance.
How else do I hear the dead in the bells

and so commit whatever praise remains.
Above the signatures, beyond the smoke.

6.

The night my father died, I lay awake
and listened to the frogs in my garden,

and I thought of a North American
song with headlights across the far field,

how they dimmed into a cold sensation
of ruin and communion, in a language

without fathers, not as we know them,
lose them. Lying in that wilderness felt

personal and not, which was its mercy.
Frogs sing, one to all, and so, to me,

when I am nowhere to be heard. So yes,
a man could feel one with the One, free

in the violent wind, and sign his poems,
breathe with a maddened need to breathe.

7.

Eyes know more about a boundary
than a mind can see. I read therefore

I blink a lot, so swift the guillotine
of shade that falls, I go a little blind.

A body breathes or it dies. It holds
its breather in, the way I held a girl

when I was a child and unconscious,
and then, as I woke up, I let her go.

Sentimentalists of chaos know so
little of their subject. A broken child

dreams of shelter, and who does not.
I dream of earth on fire in the distance.

I dream of shelter enough. I tell myself,
if only I were better. Safer, kinder.

8.

The long illness, the nervous breakdown,
the pain that tore your mother's mind

to a flock of leaves, they have returned
to tell you, the wilderness is everywhere.

And you can find comfort there because
where else. You can wheel a woman's chair

down the brief hall and pause there: this
is my world now, she says, and the woods

will give you words and never words enough.
You will see them in a window, before you

turn, past these strangers, down the hall.
I is not an I, I read. And never nothing,

I add, come nightfall, but some stained
glass of dust and tears before we name it.

9.

I knew a boy who took acid and crawled
out a window on the seventh floor.

I did that too, in a dream, and lived.
The difference between us was night

and day. Thus ambiguous at dawn.
Reading the dream as a dream is how

reading was invented. If you want to
know where a dream ends, the world

begins, ask the boy. Are clouds beyond
the window's cross so beautiful it hurts,

like joy hurled at the speed of crystal
striking a wall. Are you that unloved,

that ecstatic. Has a world against your
eye caught fire. Do you think you can fly.

10.

There is a lion in the distance. A star.
And when he roars, the heart is no one

and no one else. In a gentler season,
we all could be a little kinder, darker,

taking time in the impersonal woods
full of bird calls and carnivorous vines.

If I felt safer, less in need of shelter,
I could be the lion and the meat he eats

and the crushing beauty of the sun
that passes through the impersonal sky.

But when I wake, I am the I that wakes
inside the unseen woods that never sleep.

When I see my home from a distance,
the lords and lions are vanishing from earth.

II.

The rhinoceros before you, slaughtered
for its horn, lies disfigured, dismantled,

slow to rot beneath a stream of pincers,
suns, seizures of rain. Its magnificence

fades crowned in flies. Everything returns,
and nothing does. Everything gets eaten.

The horn capsules swallowed as a male
enhancer bear witness. There are men

who will try anything these days, and still
they wilt, they turn their faces to the wall.

The supplements they eat do nothing.
Still they eat. They swallow their prayers

and dream of better wilder lovers, girls
who whisper, *Be careful what you wish for.*

12.

With all the smoke and mirrors in the world,
I do know this. The coral reefs are dying.

Now you see them, now the skeletons
dissolve. When I was an invisible child,

I grew so frightened of the dark, I kept
my door open. Then, as I grew older,

I felt safer with it closed. Whenever
I cannot close my eyes for fear of what

I find there, I find it harder still to open.
Either way, the ocean washes in.

It takes of my blood and washes out
a little warmer. It takes the way earth takes

on the flames you see in satellite stills.
To the south, the hems of angels, burning.

13.

When my spirit broke in half and faltered,
an angel came to me and said, let me

tell you a story. Once there was a man
who so loved a woman in hell, he played

a harp to open up a passage: remember
when music blew the apples into bloom.

This was it, the first song, the song of loss.
Long before he looked back, exceeding

his given measure of control, nature's
poisons flowered through the eye and deeper.

He stood apart, just enough. Shadows
opened. Music died and lived and died

to hear the skylark answer, to see the limbs
of the lemon and the pear bow down.

14.

If a mother ever sang you to sleep,
you need no explanation, no better reason

to reply. A lullaby opens a passage,
and you fall, you sink, and when you wake,

you tear your limbs by a thousand roots
and tentacles away. I cannot tell you

where our need for mastery began.
Only that a song could frame the better

reason to sleep, and later, to awaken.
Later still, to leave your home on fire.

Oblivion reminds me, the ice is burning,
and who is not. Who has not longed to be

more radiant, then less and less, to read
in the darkening path one great longing.

15.

For the sad chorale is never sad alone.
It moves with the sure, slow provenance

of processionals and ships and somnolent
clouds that give the feathered light a place

to fall. It plows the cinders like a moon,
then carries the child in its arms to lay her

in bed and whisper something sweet,
something about a fortress in the wilderness,

what some fine day a wilderness can be.
One morning you will unlatch the glass

and breathe the leaves from the branches.
You will love a limb's measures of surrender

as you love your freedom, as *amen* loves
its tension and sigh. To ask the silence in.

16.

What I wish for the earth is a new mind
by which I mean a truer conversation

that listens close, the way a singer must
when a bird in the back of the room calls,

when she hears again the voice she dreamt,
assuming it was hers. It broke her in two,

remember. It shattered into a hundred
to join the great migrations of the south.

You were there too. You were a traveler
and carried your guitar like a language.

We were all there together. Remember.
You opened your case and birds flew out.

And the stretch of sky we took for dead
launched a thousand candles in the dark.